RANTS FROM A RACING MIND
"Chatterton's Revenge"

RANTS FROM A RACING MIND
"Chatterton's Revenge"

by

cosmo Rowley

Edited by Amie Montemurro

To:
Jared - Thank you for every night you
convinced me to stay alive.
Thank you for being as broken, divergent, and
honest with me as I've been with you.

To:
Chatterton [1752-70] - The Bristol born
virtuoso. Though citizens of two different
eras, our conversations prompted me to pursue
this expressive medium.

To:
Post-Millennial Aliens - I hope this book
offers companionship to you lost and
misunderstood souls.
You're never alone, and this book is
witness to that truth.

PHASES?

THE VOID ---------------------- 11

THE ISOLATION ----------------- 33

THE INSANITY ------------------ 55

THE VOID

I'm sad.
I want to be happy,
but I know happiness isn't a constant, so
I'm sad.

I'm sad because these rants
are my only companion.

I'm sad because I've lost interest
Interest in video games . interest in school
in family . in friends
love & life.

I'm sad because I know nothing
and nothing I know really matters in the end
but still I care . still I give
I still hope & I'm still human.

I'm sad bc i'm bored.
Life is now stale,
and the colors have turned Grey.

I'm watching a TV series
with the same storyline every episode.

My only fear about the end...is a rerun.

- 53. A DISHEARTENED RANT

Fuck!!!
I can't breathe wtf...
feels like I'm drowning and gasping for air...

ok it's getting better...
I just have to keep writing...
why tf am I crying...

MAKE IT STOP!!!

- 57. CONFUSED

The emptiness is now filling
with more space

The vacuum is getting wider
I'm getting more restless

I can't fucking inhale!
I literally just ran out of class mid lecture bc
I can't breathe...
I need water...
What I really need is oxygen

I think my heart has a polyester sleeve
It feels really hot inside

I can't stop pacing...
I can't stop moving...
But I'm running out of breath

I'm scared...
Feels like I've been spinning for hours

FUCK!!

Make it stop!!

It hurts so bad...

I just want to yell... scream... and punch
But I'm in school...
Just gotta stay cool m8

- 70. STILL CONFUSED

Wish I could care
without giving you the wrong idea.

Wish I could care
without you thinking I care too much.

Wish we could have conversations
that doesn't involve a next move.

I hate chess . I suck at chess.

I'd rather show you my cards.
All spade no hearts.
I hide my hearts underneath my sleeve.

- Dedicated to kids like me, struggling with
basic human nuances.

- 75. *SIMPLE IS SIMPLER*

We're not sick . you just don't get it...

you categorize it
give us a pill . call us crazy

Maybe you don't see it
I'll pretend I don't see it either
I can only pretend for so long
I guess I can rant for longer

Maybe you do see it
you're just not ready to stare into the abyss
you're too scared to stare into the abyss

We didn't have a choice
We didn't find it
We stumbled on it

Now we can't ignore it
It's fucking everywhere!

our relationships
our route
It's in my fucking head!

You just get to go home and ignore it
I get to go home and cry
I get to go home and hurt
I get to go home and feel

Fuck you!
I'm Jealous of you
I envy your ignorance
You don't deserve it

I wish you knew...

If you all felt our pain
you'd all wish u couldn't feel too.

- 76. MAD MEN KnOW

I can't explain it
violence seems like the best response

Over anticipation
instigated by adrenaline

Then tears of disappointment follows
Then an overwhelming feeling of shame
now tears of remorse

Then I try to fight it with violence
which only heightens the feeling
So I just accept it

That's a poor fucking explanation
but it's still the best I got

- 77. *STILL CONFUSED II*

My heart is heavy and I can't contain it
I can't stop the beating
and I can't stop the bleeding

I need air

I get this irritating feeling
as though the walls of the world is
closing in on me

I'm in the midst of a natural disaster
but nothing is going on
it's just me and my laptop

The air isn't helping like I thought it would
i'm drinking water but still thirsty
the more I breathe the more I run out of breath

I'm gonna stop writing this maybe it'll stop...

- 125. STILL CONFUSED III

I want to be free
Weightless boundless careless

I want to do less feeling and more nothing
Less reacting and more floating

Relief. clean air. new day.

Just let go...
I'm too scared...
Just let go...
It may hurt me
Just let go...
It may hurt them
Just let go...
They need me, I can't abandon them...
Just let go...
What if I'm wrong
Just let go...
Maybe I ca....

One way... Red lights.

- 126. THEN THERE WAS NOTHING

What is this...
I'm tired of guessing
The words aren't enough
The tears aren't enough
The walls aren't enough

Wilting slowly...
Dying slowly...

Understanding the absence
Digging at the wounds

I need more emptiness
I need more hopelessness
I need more nothingness

This rant is incomplete

There was something missing...
couldn't place my finger on it...

- *145. MORE EMPTY SPACES*

If you have everything
Everything means nothing

Now you want nothing
But to feel nothing

The dark clouds shadow your day
The bright stars seem so distant

You can't make wishes
So you wake up and repeat.

- *150. WHATS THE USE?*

Crying in classrooms
Deep breaths on stairways

Too many people
Lens isn't dark enough

Tears slipping thru

Crack a smile
Let em think it's all good

Be an asshole
Let em think ur no good

Talk to someone maybe
they can help you out

What can they do
past giving me another pill

Hurt some more
that'll make u heal

But u still gotta get back on set
or they'll know how u feel

- 162. SCREENPLAY TO MY LIFE

Ever cry without reason?
I'm desperate to talk to the dead
The thoughts are overwhelming

I stopped making sense in the 10th grade
My insides begun deteriorating in the 12th grade

You're all too normal . I'm uncomfortable
Curiosity continues to consume my ill-defined
existence

You think I'm weird or eccentric
I know it's insanity knocking on my door, yet
again.

I want so bad to answer that call
Yet I don't... why?

- 166. ALIEN BOY IS A MAD MAN

Do u think I discovered it too early?
I think I did...

Think it's always been there?
Think they lived their whole lives with it?

I don't think I can get past 27 like this,
I can barely make 25 lolz

Temporary fixes keep me here.
Temporary fixes don't get along with me no more.

Expiration date says (—) "what's the use?"
Relativity tells me (—) "there is no use"

Reality is false.

Death invites me on a trip
"Let's travel thru the unknown"

In Memory of Malcolm McCormick (Thank you Mac)

- 179. OBLIVION

Living a life feeling utterly useless
Writing words that'll never be more
Experiencing complex emotions you know they'll
never understand

The road ahead is foggy (and)
Dreams of tomorrow hunt you today

(So) You dwell on your mediocrity a bit longer
Wishing you had more to show while you're younger

(But) Knowing all the talent in the world won't
fix that broken soul.

You say you'd rather die early than pay patronage
to a faceless existence

Till the late night comes calling I suggest you
keep time searching for a remedy

A glue to patch your broken souls.

The World is not enough**
Your love is not enough**
Your World is not enough**

- 180. THE WORLD IS NOT ENOUGH II

I've got an empty shelve
Tried filling it with books
Tried filling it with vinyls
Tried filling it with canvas
Still empty spaces left

Tried filling it with shoes
Tried filling it with lens
Tried filling it with friends
Still empty spaces left

The empty spaces hurt me
The empty spaces hunt me
The empty spaces taunt me

How do I ask you to
help me fill the empty spaces
while maintaining the rhyme scheme ?

- 182. DR. SEUSS IS UNIMPRESSED

I swear it's been 4:59am the past 3h.
The clock stops ticking
The mind starts screaming

Only a few more hours to go...

Hid the middle 9 lines from you.
Try filling that empty space without knowing
what to fill it with.

That's how it all feels :)

- 207. MORE EMPTY SPACES PT 2

I swear it's been 4:59am the past 3h.
The clock stops ticking
The mind starts screaming

Guess it's time to put the needle on the record
Guess it's time to put the needle on the...

Not today.
Today u sit here
In the middle of this bed
In the middle of this room
Today you don't run
cosmo, today I suggest u face the night
and what troubles it brings

Only a few more hours to go...

- *208. MORE EMPTY SPACES PT 2A*

I'm not good at anything
I'm a little below average at a lot of things
But good enough at nothing...

I'm just below Joe
Puts me in an awkward spot bc fuck Joe
Serves for a good enough insecurity tho...

I'm semi forgettable
school, writing, design, humaning, film
I keep telling myself I just haven't found it...

I lied.

I'm good at masking emotions
I'm good at self deprecation
I'm good at coming off the wrong way

Just not at anything I wish I were good at.

"This piece is average af"
there's a point to be made

"This piece is really good!"
see line 12 for details. lolz.

- *223. HEY JOE*

I wish it were school. Work. Friends.
But the emptiness causes the mutilation
A growing fear that I'll never rid myself of it

Even after I amass the wealth
Even after you love me
Even after I garner enough relevance to justify
my existence

I'll still feel too empty . too unfulfilled.
Then I'll resort back to this temporary fix.

I confess:
I'm becoming permanently addicted to this
temporary fix

I confess:
I cut and burn . so I can cry and sleep

That's the only way time passes at 22
After all, time heals all... the irony.

- 227. CRASH THEN RELAPSE

THE ISOLATION

Whenever I got in trouble with mother
I always felt better when my sisters
got into trouble too
I felt less alone

I guess what I'm trying to say is
I may not say or have anything
that makes u feel better
if I did I'd be better too

You may not know how to express it in words
—— the words haven't been invented yet
but for what it's worth
I'm no better

- 122. cosmo's ISLAND

Ksa ot deracs oot m'i tub pleh deen i.
Ssenippah fo edacaf siht ni evil I.
Elpoep thiw filled dlrow a ni ylenol gnileef
yadyreve dneps I.
Etum no elihw gnilley m'i.

I need help but I'm too scared to ask. I live in this facade of happiness. I spend everyday feeling lonely in a world filled with people. I'm yelling while on mute.

- 30. HELP ME RANT

* A Rant About These Rants *

These thoughts keep me up at night,
so I write.

Can you hear it too?
I feel the dirt on my back and guilt in my heart,
when I try to ignore it.

Then I wake in the middle of the night to rant.
roaming about at 6am writing these words,
these meaningless words with no structure.

but when I write these rants,
when I give these thoughts life through my pen,
I hear silence.

Silence for the moment.
then the voices come back again,
so I keep writing.

Now the sun is setting,
distractions are wakening,
the noise is being drowned by day.

Remind me why I long for these lonely nights?

- 42. ESCAPE THE MIND

When would these lonely nights' fade?
What's the point of having people around
if you can't tell them how you feel?

I'm holding a pen in my hand
and a knife on my desk, but —
I choose the pen every time

Today I tried trading the pen for the knife
but I know you'll call me selfish
yet every fucking night I trade
my potential freedom for

H e l l   on   E a r t h.

- 54. CHOSE THE PEN

Just scrolled thru my contact list and realized
I can't text anyone how I feel right now.

I can't tell anyone,
I'm sad and can't figure out why...

I can't tell anyone,
I'm mad and can't figure out why...

I can't tell anyone,
I'm scared and can't figure out why...

I can't tell anyone,
I feel empty and can't figure out why...

I can't tell anyone,
I can't tell anyone anything
and can't figure out why...

Just scrolled thru my contact list and realized
I have no contact.

- 66. 000-000-0000

The decisions you have to make on your own
are the worst

The journey you have to travel alone
is the longest

The cross you have to carry without help
is the heaviest

The timer still ticks [8…7…6…]
The manual you got can't stop the pending
explosion [5…4…3…]
You still have to cut the wires yourself [2…1…]

- 84. Untitled II

When I have a problem
When I feel hurt
When I feel sad
When I feel pain

I do what every mentally unhealthy person does,
I keep it to myself.

When you have a problem
When you feel hurt
When you feel sad
When you feel pain

You aren't hesitant to seek comfort.

I'm comforted by my pain so in time,
I can become numb.

I hate how you deal with your emotions.

- 90. HEALTHY SINS

Loneliness is the match that lights it all...

Then comes the anger derived from frustration

the sadness birthed from envy

Confusion is the glue that ties
the Anger to the sadness

I had more to say
but it doesn't matter...

You couldn't even understand the first 5 lines.

- 107. *SPARK OF LONELINESS*

I was scared I'll fuck it up
I got too close
You got too close
You tried to understand but failed
I was easing your pain... for when I leave
I missed the pain I felt from the loneliness
I got bored... I get bored a lot

Use any of these
when you get cold and distant
but can't seem to explain why
to the people that love you

- 124. THE EXPLANATIONS

I needed a friend
and no one was there

You just didn't seem to care enough
I just didn't want to burden you too much

Figured I could just cry and get over it
I'm getting tired of crying,
but I'm still not over it

I shld'nt blame you for me not opening up
I blame you for me not opening up

You didn't ask if I was ok enough
Maybe u did once or twice
but never asked a third time

Maybe u did ask a third time
but I could see your growing frustration
at my silence

Your frustration only helped me
decide to keep it all locked up

It hurts
because I would never stop asking
"Are you ok?"

- 128. ARE YOU OK?

The sun is too bright
I've run out of words

Melancholy created the rift
but gave me my only friend

Now I find myself a gypsy,
wandering thru life

An alien following a ghost.
I cannot explain what you cannot see

So I write these meaningless words
and make these shitty paintings

In an attempt to understand the alien within
and describe the ghost I pursue

Remain till your muse departs
remain then till your ghost departs
be it to the world beyond...

In memory of Thomas "Rowley" Chatterton.

- *129. CHATTERTON IS cosmo*

A lonely red balloon
floating in the blue skies

How close to the blue can it float
without exploding
How close to the blue can I float
without exploding

How tight is the string
holding its lips shut
How tight is the string
holding my lips shut

Then I look down
and see the strings puppeteering you

The strings on your arms legs heads chest
I think I'll take my chances...

A lonely red balloon
floating into deeper blue skies

- 130. LONELY RED BALLOON

Winter is coming
I'm beginning to feel the weight of the mornings
like the night before

The fall was short lived
but long enough for me to find myself
in the harshest of winters

I feel the sting of loneliness
like the frostbites on my finger tips

My pants?
ripped and Ill prepared

My coat?
thick enough for me to hide
but too heavy to carry around

My vans . too thin
my mind . too thick

Shelving Thalia...
shelving my heart

Just long enough till the tears turn to rain
Just long enough till winter is over.

- *132. WITHER IN THE WINTER PT 2*

You make me feel alone
I'm not alone

I don't mean to hurt myself
I just fell for the trap
Now I feel alone

So I hurt myself
Idk why
It's a calm

I wish you never see this one
But ik someday you will

hopefully it's not too late
Hopefully you don't just see a "sad kid"

- 151. SAD KIDS

Is it ok if I cry to you?
I know it's not man like...

Is it ok if I open up to you?
I know it's not man like...

Is it ok if I scream to you?
I know it's not man like...

Filled with emotion
Overcome with sadness
Crying on train rides
Reminiscing on nostalgia.

Fighting the awkwardness
Hating the weirdness
Masking the misery

I feel everything and everything hurts.

Wish you loved me like I love you.
But you don't.

So all that's left is hate...
hate birthed from rejection.

- *156. HURT FEELINGS*

You travelled too far from home...

Interaction is hard
Rejection is cold

Emotions rage like the rising storms

Restless soul hurting over electric guitar rifts

Train couldn't take you home
so the thoughts linger

Alone in the night
u nurse ur wounds the wrong way

Music becomes background noise to the pain

Drown the pain in tears and aggression

All out of tears
so blood begun to drip

Now imagine it all never happened.

- 168. HOMESICK ALIEN

Not enough processing power
Data overload
System crashing
Thoughts distorted

"sense making hard It's"
"harder explain Even to"

Tired of the overwhelming emotions
Even more tiring to write about

[root@cosmo ~]$ sudo shutdown -r now.

Reload.
Back to basics

cd ~

Hide it all from urself
Backed up in the cloud
Problems for the subconscious

ENOSPC

- 214. HUMAN ERROR 28

USE THIS BLANK SPACE TO EXHALE

USE THIS BLANK SPACE TO EXPRESS

Put the needle on a record and let the story
begin...

Normal had me feeling worthless
So I locked my phone and shut the door

Spent the next 2 weeks living with paranoia.

We had a lot of one sided conversations

Paranoia:
You're the chosen one living amongst
Primates. A reincarnation of the messiah

Also Paranoia:
You're just a mad man grabbing at straws.
We all know ur a fraud,
stay here as to not scare them off.

Designed more art to cover the thoughts,
guess that's why they call it Cover Art.

But more Casagemas less Picasso.
Spent the next 2 weeks escaping via photoshop.

I'll paint the picture:

Pretty red foreground
complimented with rough scars and grainy
background.

So much imposter syndrome
I increased the opacity and heightened the noise.

Pretty sure the two weeks are up.

Saying my goodbyes to paranoia
(what a confusing guy smh)

Taking the needle off the record,
this is where the story ends...

but now I got blood stains on my vinyl.
Don't you just hate being this clumsy? Lolz

- 240. PARANOID ANDROID: THE WRITING

THE INSANITY

1. Become aware of the value of existence
   or lack thereof.

2. This discovery will leave you dissatisfied
   and unwilling to enjoy the construct.

3. Your inability to enjoy the construct
   will make u unimpressed and no doubt
   bring about boredom.

4. Bored and unimpressed,
   you will resort to isolation.

5. The gap you have created
   between urself and society will
   get so wide u'd forget how to human.
   Soon you'd begin loosing your wits...

sanity slips like sand slips thru an open palm.
   .

   .

   .

- 184. 5 STEPS TO LUNACY

Don't wanna jinx it but...
it's been pretty calm up here lately.

Is it weird that I might miss the chaos?
That I feel incomplete.

I feel even more a John Doe...

- 59. WHITE NOISE

I'm loosing my wits, like the days
the mask is slipping off, of my face
The winter like the night . no escape

I hate it, but it gets comfortable
under that blanket.

told my doctor I can't skate in the winter
the slopes are slippery
and the air dries my blood

he told me to find
another source of escape

I then had a quick daydream

I burst out in tears
After I stabbed him repeatedly

I wither in the winter
Spring can't come soon enough
so I can skate towards the sun
and fall on the other side.

- 61. WITHER IN THE WINTER

It's happening again...

I want to grab him by the neck
squeeze till he stops breathing

I want to drag him on the ground
pummel him till I see him bleed

I'm shaking . literally twitching
heart is racing . the adrenaline is amazing!

I can't hurt him
but I want to soo bad.

how long can I stop myself?
how long can I stay sane?

I need help . I need a reason
Tell me — what's wrong with me?

Please !!
I need to hurt u.
I need to feel pain.

give me a reason to.

- 65. MR. RAGER

We're not sick . you just don't get it .

you categorize it
give us a pill . call us crazy

Maybe you don't see it
I'll pretend I don't see it either

I can only pretend for so long
I guess I can rant for longer

Maybe you do see it
you're just not ready
to stare into the abyss

you're too scared
to stare into the abyss

We didn't have a choice
We didn't find it
We stumbled on it

Purple thoughts...
I've pictured your crime scene
I've painted your crime scene

Purple thoughts...
Don't lean on them, it may spill over

Purple thoughts...
Black bathrooms .
Steaming showers .
Foggy mirrors .
It steps out of the tub
Steady stream of dark blood dripping from both
wrists

You barged in
You see the tormented smile on it's face
You see the fiery spark of insanity in its eyes
You see the daring tilt of it's head

Purple thoughts...
You count sheep
It pictures taking that foot off the ledge

Purple thoughts
I'm using you
You're just writing material
You don't matter

Purple thoughts spilling over...

- 141. PURPLE THOUGHTS

Airplane on
.

.

.

I feel the need to cause pain
I feel the need to feel pain

Airplane off
.

.

.

I turned off airplane while I caused me pain
I hoped u'd call while I caused me pain

Now I need a bandage
Try helping without helping

- 144. ANOTHER HOLE IN THE WALL

Playing in my own vomit
Bathing in my own tears

The tears disguises itself in the shower
so now it's one n' the same

Filling the tub till I drown
Hot enough so I'm numb

Now I can't feel my right arm
but I'm still here

The shower head bids me goodbye
My eye lids bid me good night

Everything's moving but time...

Sinking slow . Breathing fast

Head hung sideways impatiently waiting
for the light behind the blackness

It never came.

Naked skin pressed on the living room floor

Woke up with nothing but blurred vision

Now starring at the ceiling
waiting for the sky behind it to collapse

- 170. ALIEN BOY'S TRIP TO NOTHINGNESS

Tough
/təf/
adjective
Strong enough to withstand adversity

Skin
/skin/
noun
The thin layer of tissue forming the natural
outer covering of the body

i.e., "Knife isn't sharp enough... Only leaves
scars. No cuts."

- 175. TOUGH SKIN

Dashing down the steep n' bumpy hills of insanity
Form is wrong. Your knees weren't bent enough
Hold on tight! hold on tight to nothing (lmao)

You're not crying
It's just the wind in ur eyes

Know ur headed on collision course at the bottom
Fuck it. Brace yourself!
Happy endings are overrated anyways :)

I'm bad at human

- 185. BAD HUMAN . DO BETTER

Still peeling my skin...
hoping for a new one underneath

Disappointed...
like when there was nothing
under the Christmas tree

Readjusting...
like when you gotta act like
u knew all along

Remind yourself...
Like when bad kids get detention

Hope is cruel . Alien boy is alright
Hope is cruel . Alien boy is alright
Hope is cruel . Alien boy is alright
Hope is cruel . Alien boy is alright

Hope is cruel . I'm not alright

Repeat.

- 190. RINSE N' REPEAT

Don't worry bout me
I only cut a little

I'm more of a burn myself kinda crazy
Occasionally I do try oxygen deprivation

When it gets really bad I go full on psycho
Full on Kurt Cobain... Montage Of Heck
Full on The Wall... One of My Turns
Full on Kid Cudi... CONFUSED!

But it's really not that bad
I just hurt enough to cry bloody red

There are others out there way worse
Someone shld help them

I wanna help them
Can't help them if I'm gone

Someone shld help me
Wish I were ready to help me. Lolz

The blood is drying on the razor
The Shine on You riff is at its peak

I gotta go hurt a little more...

- 195. HEALTHY SINS PT 3

The blade was my pick
My skin was the string

My strums ever so slow
wanted to feel every second of the music
Blood flowing out was a Van Gogh

Couldn't tell pain from bliss

Calm and drowsy
Euphoric and intoxicating

Dressing the wounds is the best part
Feel the rush . Feel the butterflies

The cool sting of alcohol to the skin

Fulfilling...

- 199. WARNING: DON'T TRY THIS AT HOME :)

Wrist bleeding of inspiration
Took a pic to remember the feeling

Vivid warm or dramatic?
There's some irony in using a filter
Find it.

Vivid warm really shows the scars
The dead red really pops in dramatic

I'll prob go with dramatic

Sometimes I think I'm too dramatic
Sometimes I think it's really not that bad
Sometimes I think I'm overreacting

But if it's really not that bad...
Why does my wrist always bleed of inspiration?

PS. I swear I really fought the urge this time

- 204. POST-MILLENNIAL VAN GOGH

Scared of both life n' death

"Keep me in limbo" — I asked

"Let me travel between worlds" — I begged

The answer remains no.
Still too human to do the impossible

\\

Found a tight corner in the tub
sterilize my thoughts in boiling water
Let my brown skin turn purple

If I can't be alive n' dead
Let me feel alive n' dead

- 213. MID-NIGHT BRAIN DAMAGE

I feel the need to write all my thoughts.

I get a bit dizzy in populated areas,
that may ruin our plans for the night.

My desire to sit in a specific seat
will get annoying.

Overly sensitive to light and sound.

I re-read and extensively annotate
the same page in a book.

I often count or repeat
the same random phrase in my head,
for minutes at a time.

Sleeping is difficult.

I don't know how to stop talking to myself
and it gets pretty loud.

I might randomly stop
saying words mid conversa...

I'd often go on tangents
and lose my train of thought.

I will ignore you a lot . I can't help it lolz

- 218. PRODROME V2

Been 3 days since I slept
Mind's been racing with no line in sight.

I wish so bad I could explain to u how it feels
I want so bad to crawl back inside my skin

just a moment of silence will do...

It always starts with
what shld be simple thoughts
But my mind doesn't let me
think simple thoughts

There has to be more... ask questions
The hole goes deeper... look further

Obsession is insanity
I'm rocking back n forth in an empty bathroom

Obsession is insanity
It's very loud in this empty bathroom

"Everything is Nothing"
I shld write that on my skin
so I don't forget

I shld've never gone out
without my hoodie

- 220. LUNACY

My finger tips smell like bloody bandaids

I know u never bleed so
think of burnt plastic,
rusted iron, and kerosene

Last night they were stained with acrylic brown

I know u paint too
wish we painted for
the same reasons

I shld go wash the smell off my hands
but sitting here feels much easier

Dedicated to May Rio from Poppies

- *224. ANYONE?*

I wish it were School. Work. Friends.
But the emptiness causes the mutilation
A growing fear that I'll never rid myself of it

Even after I amass the wealth
Even after you love me
Even after I garner enough relevance to justify
my existence

I'll still feel too empty . too unfulfilled
Then I'll resort back to this temporary fix

*   *   *

I confess:
I'm becoming permanently addicted
to this temporary fix

I confess:
I cut and burn . so I can cry and sleep
That's the only way time passes at 22

After all, time heals all... the irony.

- 227. CRASH THEN RELAPSE

USE THIS BLANK SPACE TO INHALE

USE THIS BLANK SPACE TO REFLECT

Doing my time . Earning my stripes
Got 60 of em on my wrist to prove it

All my hoodies soaked on the sleeves
been swimming in deep red . That's a blood bath

Fuck you and ur frivolous woes
I'm about to add to ur salt . Bruise to ur ego

Feeling like GOD again
Your savior . Your destroyer

You're not worth my breath
That bar was literal

Toxic masculinity
More like toxic humanity

End the sentence at 23. Fuck 25-life
More on that later...

Real courage is laughing while u bleed
That bar was literal

"A villain will save your world."

You will not understand these words
How pathetic.

You need structure & rhyme schemes . The illusion

We could never fit the box
We never plugged in the socket

I could say more but line 13.

- 239. LINE-13

It all starts after that last "lolz" text...

Then the weight of the winter
starts creeping up

Soon enough I'm too cold
Too cold to speak . Too cold to eat

All I want is nothing
All my stares are blank

as I reach for the silver blade
carefully hidden away.

Eyes filled with life just 3 hours ago...

Now dried up and withered
like everything else around.

Not another one... not another winter.

- 243. WITHER IN THE WINTER PT 4

Ever dipped ur toes in the water?
Just to sea how deep it is

Cut ur wrist and daydream
Just to feel how much it hurts

Sip dye and cry at night
Just to taste how bad it gets

She said this feeling is a moment,
and it'll pass

I said this moment feels like eternity,
and I'm at an impasse

- 245. MERE SIMILES & METAPHORS

I think I'm gonna die
I think I'm gonna die before 2021,
and I can't avoid it

I think I'm gonna die
I think I'm probably gonna die today,
Most likely right now

I swear I tried.

Chatterton would be disappointed
But I'm not made for this world,
Neither was he

Let's play make believe
Humor me, one last time

Let's call this rit dye arsenic
Call me "Chatterton's Revenge" one last time

Let me go like the romantic did,
to a place where everything is nothing

A place my delusions won't follow

- 246. FAREWELL COSMO

USE THIS BLANK SPACE TO LEARN

USE THIS BLANK SPACE TO GROW

Reader FYI:

As you read, you noticed the peculiar use of punctuation
and text speech within the syntax — such as repeated patterns of
"..." or "u".

You will also find the use of strong language, urban vernacular,
and the inclusion of meme/troll culture.
It is important to me that you realize this is no oversight
but an attempt to evolve the art that is written language.

William Shakespeare didn't write in the same manner
Thomas Chatterton did. CS Lewis certainly didn't write
in the voice of Shakespeare.
In each era, a new pattern of speech was formed,
and each brought with it an evolution of written expression.

It is wise to learn the foundation, but why create a foundation
if you don't intend to build on it?
I am birthed to a generation influenced by
Rick & Morty, IOT, and Kanye West.
I intend to write like it.